To:

_____

From:

_____

Date:

_____

Draw Near to Me

A Creative
Devotional Journal

Draw Near to Me

INGRID JEFFERS
Oakland, California

"Draw near to God, and He will draw near to you."
– James 4:8

TABLE OF CONTENTS

ACKNOWLEDGMENTS

GOD: Thank you for trusting me with Your seed.

COLLEEN JEFFERS: You are the most amazing woman I know. Thank you for supporting and encouraging every creative, challenging, and crazy idea of my heart.

SANIYAH JEFFERS: Thank you for being a brilliant answer from God. You inspire me to dream more, explore more, and love more.

TATIANA USSERY: Thank you for listening to me talk about this book nearly every day for the past seven months. Your faithfulness is beautiful. Your friendship is priceless.

DAWN HUMPHREY: Your creativity and passion for the gospel taught me to see beyond the numbers. Thank you for investing in my life and modeling what it means to be a dreamer and a leader.

PREFACE

I'm not ashamed to say that I actively pursue fun and creative ways to maintain and deepen my relationship with God. That's how this book was born. In the summer of 2015, I was on a ten-chapter-per-day Bible reading plan. It was amazing to see how the Bible is so interconnected—but I was getting tired of the routine. That's when I decided to switch it up and start a 31-Day Scripture Art Challenge.

Every day at 5:00 a.m., I would text a verse from Scripture to about 25 people. They would meditate on the verse and create a drawing based upon the Scripture. Taking 31 days to have our devotional time revolve around making Scripture art with God was a major step of faith for nearly everyone, and especially for me.

Even though I felt there was something powerful to be learned by coming to God in a childlike way, I still prayed earnestly that God would meet us. Most of us had been conditioned to believe that quiet time consisted of a Bible, silence, and prayer on our knees. This was a significant shift from the norm.

When we finally came together at the end of the 31 days, it was evident that the time we spent with God creating art transformed our hearts. Thinking over the daily Scriptures, asking Him questions, and listening to His responses drew us closer to Him. We understood His character and love for us in greater measure. The whole experience left us excited about what the future could hold.

In the spring of 2016, friends began to ask me if I was going to host the challenge again. I had no idea that people were expecting it to be an annual event, but I was delighted to oblige. As I began to prepare, I realized that a book was forming. Every step I took, I felt the Holy Spirit giving me specific instructions from how He wanted the content structured, to fresh insight into the Scriptures.

In those loud moments, asking God why was I writing this book, He spoke to me and said, "Those who learn to interact with Me like a child are creating the foundation for miracles in their lives." That's when I realized that God was using creativity to help us get to know Him as Father. If we built a relationship with God as Father, we would then have to recognize our identities as His sons and daughters, and with that, the rewards and responsibilities. Unknowingly, I had already tapped into this truth, and it fueled me to live a life of miracles.

Looking back, I see that the 31-Day Scripture Art Challenge helped many of us embrace a lifestyle of risk, to show people that Jesus cares and loves them outrageously. We became more vocal with our faith, by encouraging strangers through prophetic words and God's good thoughts toward them. We were more eager to lay hands on the sick and believe and see their full recovery. Our hearts had been changed, and engrained upon them was a sense of trust that God could use us to do more than we could ever imagine. All of this came forth by using creativity as the vehicle to build a stronger relationship with God as our amazing, trustworthy, and loving Father. The power found in this Father-daughter/son relationship surprised me more than anything else that took place. But, it really shouldn't have.

When the disciples asked Jesus how to pray, Jesus taught them in Matthew 6:9 to approach God as sons and daughters. Above every other attribute that makes God who He is, we are first to remember that He is our Father, and when we pray, we are talking to our Dad—not some detached, supreme being in the clouds. Living from this identity allows us to be powerful ambassadors of the gospel and conduits for the miraculous.

When we know who we are and whose we are, God's miracle-working power can flow through us. Our Father already knows us; now He wants us to know Him.

It's my goal to help raise up, launch, and support a generation of believers who are confident in who they are, know their purpose, and know their God. Together, and with God's help, we can change the world.

INTRODUCTION

Draw Near to Me is a creative devotional journal for people who want to have fun with God while being transformed by His love, empowered by His presence, and captivated by His heart to reconcile humanity to Himself.

Imagine talking to God like a little child who is sitting in the lap of their affectionate, supportive, and trustworthy parent—sharing about the smallest details of your day that brought you delight or made you laugh. God, your Father, wants those moments with you. He also wants to hear about the rough parts of your day, so that He can give you guidance and encouragement. Your Papa is eager to discuss your dreams, heal your hurts, fill you with hope, and launch you into passion-filled purpose.

Before we get started, let's discuss the biggest concern most folks have about drawing: *I don't know how to draw; I'm not an artist.* Well, don't worry; this journal doesn't require you to be. You are free to take chances, make mistakes, and get messy! There is no need to filter your art or your thoughts in this journal. Be authentically you.

When we create from a place of honesty, using our God-given abilities, our Papa smiles. Creativity is His idea. He's the Creator, and He made you in His image. Therefore, you are a creator by birth.

This creative gift that we have causes the walls, the masks, and the roadblocks to our true feelings and not-so-hidden thoughts to come down because it's fueled by emotions. It leaves us vulnerable and open to receiving the whole counsel of God, allowing for the landscape of our hearts and relationships to be made whole. This wholeness is found in God, and He promises that if we draw near to Him, He will draw near to us (James 4:8).

It's my prayer that this creative devotional journal will help you deepen your relationship with the Father and bring a new level of fun and intimacy to your time with God. Prepare yourself to be surrounded by color, spending your days creating and resting in your Papa's arms.

SMALL GROUP GUIDANCE

When we link up with other people, the potential to be more productive, creative, and motivated increases exponentially. See if you can get together a group of folks who are interested in reading with you. You'll be thankful for the support and the encouragement that comes from spending time with other like-minded believers. The group you form doesn't have to be big. Where two or three are gathered as followers of Jesus, He is there with them (Matthew 18:20).

In an effort to help you get the most out of this creative devotional journal, *Draw Near to Me* has been divided into eight sections. Each section covers a specific topic for one week, which includes six devotion days and one Growing Closer day. After completing six of the daily devotions on your own, I hope that on the seventh day your group can meet to discuss the Growing Closer questions.

Draw Near to Me has been organized in such a way to take you on a journey. Each week you will build upon the growth of the previous weeks, with a focus on the treasures to be discovered in the current week.

Week 1 will look at the fact that every person has been created and chosen by God to live with purpose, and how our lives should reflect this truth. In Week 2, we focus on the doctrine of the Godhead and learn more about the Father, the Son, and the Holy Spirit. We then transition to Week 3 and explore what it means to love and be loved. In Week

4, we take a look at what prevails when love is absent, and address the issue of dealing with sin. This is followed by a week of learning about God's protection and provision in Week 5. Then we move into Week 6, where we discuss our significance and purpose as given to us by God. In Week 7, we zone in on the equipping and empowering stage of every believer's life. Lastly, in Week 8, we focus on being unleashed and released into a great adventure with God.

Throughout the eight-week journey, I provide you with penetrating questions and guide you with prayer and drawing prompts to help facilitate a conversation between you and God.

SMALL GROUP AGENDA

Following a small group agenda is a great way to gain confidence as a small group leader. You might not always follow it, but an agenda can be helpful in getting started.

Below you will find a suggested outline, but feel free to tweak it to meet your needs.

DRAW NEAR TO ME AGENDA:

1. Welcome & prayer
2. Dance break
   - This devotional is about having fun with God. Start your small group with a dance break.
3. Connection question
   - Ask a question that allows each person to share what has happened in their lives since the last meeting.
   - The question can be broad or specific. For example, a broad question might be, "How has your week been?" while a specific question might be, "What risk did you take this week to serve someone well?"
   - The connection questions should allow for people to be

open about their blessings and challenges. This will help deepen relationships within the group.

4. Tell of God's goodness

   - Ask each person to share something good God has done for them in the past week.

   - Thank God for these praise reports.

5. Pair share

   - Have each person find a partner and share a meaningful "DRAW" entry from the past week, and its significance.

6. Growing Closer discussion questions

7. Pray for one another

8. Thank God

BASIC ART SUPPLIES

To start, try using art supplies you already own. As you begin the process of creating, you will get a feel for what other tools you may want for future drawings. Eventually, you will figure out which tools and medium best suit your self-expression.

Below you will find a list of basic supplies to get you started.

Required:

- Journal (6" x 9" or bigger) – If you want to paint or use watercolors, purchase a mixed media journal
- Colored Pencils or Markers – Two colors
- Pens – Two colors (Permanent ink won't smear if it gets wet)
- Scissors
- Glue
- Collage Material

Optional:

- Watercolors
- Acrylic paint
- Paint brushes
- Ruler
- Additional color pencils, pens and markers

How to Use this Book

Draw Near to Me contains eight weeks of daily devotions and Growing Closer questions.

Your daily devotion will include a combination of questions, prayer prompts, the drawing prompt, and other instructions. You will also have a space to write. I have found it helpful to use this space to jot down my responses, my prayers, things I'm thankful for, my hopes, and any other ideas that come to mind.

Journaling your thoughts and responses can happen very easily. One word or sentence is just as powerful as one paragraph or page of writing, when it means something to you.

To complete the drawing prompt, I suggest using a mixed media journal which will allow you the freedom to use paints, watercolors, and markers for your creations.

Fill the pages with your thoughts and with color. Highlight sections that speak to your spirit or challenge you, and of course write your responses in the spaces provided. The more you engage with the devotions, the deeper the impact of the message.

You will also have a set of weekly Growing Closer questions for small group discussions. For further details please refer to page 9.

Drawing Prompt Instructions

Each "DRAW" section is created to work in conjunction with that day's devotion, but you can deviate from the plan and create and write as you are being led. I encourage you to always err on the side of freedom, rather than compliance.

If God shares something more with you after you complete your "DRAW," take time to write down what He says.

Example #1

DRAW: Girlish laughter

If you receive a prompt that's a noun, verb, or adverb, draw what comes to mind when you read the word in light of that day's devotion. Ask God to show you.

Example #2

DRAW: What does it look like to grow?

If you receive a question prompt, draw your answer to the question in light of that day's devotion. Ask God to show you.

Example #3

DRAW: Create a couch and draw your three favorite people sitting on the couch.

If you receive a prompt that gives you instructions, please follow the instructions and draw your answer in light of that day's devotion. Ask God to guide you.

MIND MAP
INSTRUCTIONS

The concept of Mind Mapping was invented by Tony Buzan. It's a visual technique that encourages creativity and increases understanding.

1. Start off with a blank page. Make sure its orientation is landscape.
2. Place a photograph or draw an image in the center of the page.
3. Attach a key word that represents your main idea.
4. Think of ideas that can be extracted from the main idea. Come up with three to seven points.
5. For each new idea, create a curvy branch that extends from the main idea.
6. Label each new branch with your idea and create an associated image.
7. Continue this process (follow steps four through six) for each new image and key word.
8. Be sure to doodle and use colors throughout.
9. Create at least three levels of branches.
10. You can now fill in the Mind Map with questions and additional details that come to mind. Connect these thoughts to the branches in a creative way.

For examples, search for Mind Map on the internet.

God Thought Instructions

1. Get a pen, paper, and Bible.

2. Pray for the Holy Spirit to guide you in all truth (John 16:13 and John 14:26). Ask the Holy Spirit to teach you the meaning of the Scripture and how you can apply it to your life.

3. Make sure the paper's orientation is landscape.

4. Write your Scripture out in the middle of the paper.

5. For ten minutes, write all the thoughts that come to mind regarding the Scripture, including definitions for specific words, other Scriptures, connections, images, etc.

6. Connect these thoughts to the specific parts of the Scripture that are being addressed using lines, shapes and doodles.

7. Dig deeper. Write for five more minutes.

8. Now take five minutes to answer the following questions:

    - What does this Scripture tell me about God?

    - What does this Scripture tell me about man?

    - What does this Scripture tell me about myself?

9. Thank God for the word you received.

For examples, search #getthegodthought on the internet.

Draw Near to Me

"True freedom is not choice or lack of constraint, but being what you are meant to be. Humans were created in the image of God. True freedom, then, is not found in moving away from that image but only in living it out."
— **St. Augustine**

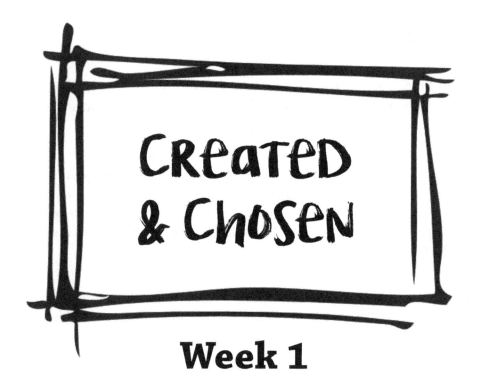

Week 1

DAY 1

Fruitfulness

"You didn't choose me. I chose you. I appointed you to go and produce lasting fruit, so that the Father will give you whatever you ask for, using my name." — **John 15:16, NLT**

The Bible often refers to people as trees that bear either good or bad fruit. In Luke 6:43-45, Jesus tells us that every tree is known by its fruit. Fruit is a symbolic representation of the visible expression of God's power working in you. The evidence of this inward work is shown in the fruit your life produces.

1. List five fruits you want to produce in your life (e.g., mended relationship, celibacy, perseverance, love, patience, hope, miracles).
2. Ask Jesus what fruits He wants you to have.
3. Thank God that He has already provided everything you need to live a godly life (2 Peter 1:2-3).
4. Thank God that He has empowered you to lead a life of fruitfulness.
5. Ask your Father to help you partner with Him to produce lasting fruit in your life.
6. Pray for strength and God's help for the journey ahead.

DRAW: A tree that is producing good fruit; you are the tree.

CReaTeD & ChoSeN

DAY 2

God's Masterpiece

"For we are God's masterpiece. He has created us anew in Christ Jesus, so we can do the good things he planned for us long ago."
— Ephesians 2:10, NLT

Before Christ, we were covered in the filth of sin; we were far from a masterpiece. However, because of the blood of Jesus and His death, burial, and resurrection, we have been transformed into a beautiful work of art.

1. Thank God for making you His masterpiece.
2. Ask God to highlight for you how He sees you. When God shows you this, it might happen in a variety of ways. You might receive an impression in your mind, receive a thought, have a feeling, see something with your eyes, hear words, or see words. These are just a few of the ways God communicates with His children. Be sure to remember this as you go through the rest of the devotional.
3. Write what He says.

DRAW: Create a frame using words and images to describe what God loves about you and what makes you His masterpiece. Place your photo in the middle.

CREATED & CHOSEN

DAY 3

▶ ▶ ▶ ▶ ▶ ▶ ▶ ▶ ▶ ▶ ▶

Known and Planned

"Thank you for making me so wonderfully complex! Your work-manship is marvelous—how well I know it. You watched me as I was being formed in utter seclusion, as I was woven together in the dark of the womb. You saw me before I was born. Every day of my life was recorded in your book. Every moment was laid out before a single day had passed." **— Psalm 139:14-16, NLT**

1. Thank God that He is your Maker.
2. Thank God that He is the reason why you are living.
3. Thank your Father that He knows your life moment by moment.
4. Thank your Father that He has a plan for your life.
5. Ask Him to guard your heart and mind with His peace as you discover His plan (Isaiah 26:3).
6. Yesterday, we learned that our Papa has already planned the good things we are to do in this life. Ask Him what He has planned for you to do? Be sure to write down at least one thing. God is not silent toward His children, He wants to speak with you and He will. You were created to hear His voice.
7. Thank God that everything He wants you to do will be done; that you will finish well (Philippians 2:13).

DRAW: An open book with the good works you will accomplish written in it.

CREATED & CHOSEN

DAY 4

Abba, Father

"And because we are his children, God has sent the Spirit of his Son into our hearts, prompting us to call out, 'Abba, Father.' Now you are no longer a slave but God's own child. And since you are his child, God has made you his heir." — **Galatians 4:6-7, NLT**

1. Thank God for your elevation in status from slave to heir.
2. Ask your Father what rights come with being an heir.
3. Ask your Father what responsibilities come with being an heir.
4. Pray that the slave mentality of lack, of poverty, of ignorance, of insignificance would be broken off your life right now in the name of Jesus.
5. Pray that your mind would be reconditioned to understanding your place as a son or daughter.
6. Pray that you step into your God-given position as a prince or princess in the Kingdom of your Papa.
7. Pray that you become stirred up by the Holy Spirit to know your significance to the world.

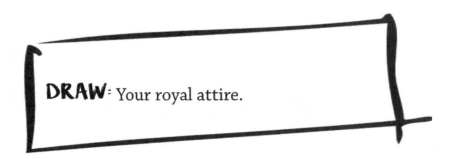

DRAW: Your royal attire.

CREATED & CHOSEN

DAY 5

Inheritance

"For his Spirit joins with our spirit to affirm that we are God's children. And since we are his children, we are his heirs. In fact, together with Christ we are heirs of God's glory. But if we are to share his glory, we must also share his suffering."
— Romans 8:16-17, NLT

God's Spirit lives in us and confirms that we are God's children. Don't overlook how special this is and how set apart this makes us. As co-heirs with Jesus, we will inherit everything in heaven and in earth, in time and outside of time, because we are children of God (Hebrews 1:2).

1. Thank God that His Spirit lives in you and declares that you are God's child.
2. Thank God that He has made you a co-heir to everything.
3. Ask your Papa to show you the mystery of your inheritance.

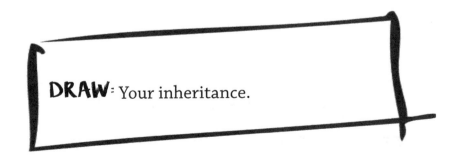

DRAW: Your inheritance.

CREATED & CHOSEN

DAY 6

Imitate God

"Imitate God, therefore, in everything you do, because you are his dear children." — **Ephesians 5:1, NLT**

1. Do you have any habits that don't show your true identity as a child of God?
   - If yes, write those habits down.
   - Ask God to change your nature and remove these habits far from you.
   - Ask God to let His light shine through you and cause your actions and thoughts to reflect His good nature.

2. Paul understood the importance and power of godly mentorship. That's why he told believers in Corinth to imitate him as he imitates Christ (1 Corinthians 11:11). Do you need to get new mentors?
   - Ask God to connect you with spiritual, career, and life mentors who follow Jesus with their words and in their actions.

3. Who are you modeling your life after (e.g., God, family, friends, spiritual leaders, politicians, educators, businessmen, etc.)?
   - Ask God to show you which role models He approves of specifically.

DRAW: One of God's characteristics that you want to imitate.

CREATED & CHOSEN

DAY 7

Created & Chosen

Growing Closer
Discussion Questions

1. Why do you think God places such a strong emphasis on our adoption as His children?

2. What benefits do we have as children of God?

3. How should our actions and attitudes be influenced by our identity as God's children?

4. What impact, if any, should our identity have on the people in our work places, schools, and communities?

"Now that doctrine of the Trinity often seems a very perplexing subject. And no wonder; I for one should be very much surprised if when the truth about God is reached we should not find something which is very perplexing to human minds and something which betrays the poverty of human speech. I expect the truth about the infinite God will always tax the fullest resources of finite minds and tongues and still leave men wondering, pondering and adoring."

— **Robert Drummond**

Week 2

DAY 8

Uniquely Qualified

In Job 38, God begins to lay out the case for why He is uniquely qualified to run the universe.

1. Read Job 38.
2. Read Job's response in Job 42:1-6.
3. What is your response to God's questions?
4. How does this chapter impact your view of God?

God's questions and cross-examination would leave any of us stammering for words. Our collective understanding comes nowhere near His infinite knowledge and wisdom.

DRAW: How do you feel after reading the passages in Job?

THE FATHER, THE SON, & THE HOLY SPIRIT

DAY 9

God's Beauty

"There is no one like the God of Israel. He rides across the heavens to help you, across the skies in majestic splendor."
— **Deuteronomy 33:26, NLT**

1. Thank God that He is a present help in times of trouble (Psalm 46:1).
2. How does it feel to know that God answers your cries for help personally?
3. Ask the Lord to show you His majestic splendor.
4. What do you see?

DRAW: God's majestic splendor.

THE FATHER, THE SON, &
THE HOLY SPIRIT

DAY 10

The Father's Happiness

"So don't be afraid, little flock. For it gives your Father great happiness to give you the Kingdom." — **Luke 12:32, NLT**

1. Thank God for being your Father.
2. Thank God for giving you the Kingdom—righteousness, peace, and joy in the Holy Spirit (Romans 14:17).
3. Ask God to show you what His great happiness looks like.
4. How does this image make you feel?

DRAW: The Father's great happiness.

THE FATHER, THE SON, & THE HOLY SPIRIT

DAY II

The Advocate

"But the Advocate, the Holy Spirit, whom the Father will send in my name, will teach you all things and will remind you of everything I have said to you." — **John 14:26, NIV**

The Holy Spirit has many roles, but His primary role is to bear witness to, or back up the testimony of Jesus Christ in the earth by empowering believers.

1. Thank the Holy Spirit for teaching you everything you need to know to avoid sin.
2. Thank the Holy Spirit for convicting you of thoughts and actions that don't line up with what Jesus teaches in the Scriptures.
3. Thank the Holy Spirit for empowering you to live a life that glorifies Jesus.
4. Ask the Holy Spirit to make your heart more sensitive to His voice and guidance.
5. Ask the Holy Spirit to strengthen you to live like Jesus.

DRAW: A student of the Holy Spirit.

THE FATHER, THE SON, & THE HOLY SPIRIT

DAY 12

The Son and the Father

"The Son radiates God's own glory and expresses the very character of God, and he sustains everything by the mighty power of his command. When he had cleansed us from our sins, he sat down in the place of honor at the right hand of the majestic God in heaven." **— Hebrews 1:3, NLT**

Jesus was the exact re-presentation of God when He walked the earth (Hebrews 1:3 and John 5:19). Every characteristic that we assign to Jesus, we can credit to God the Father. Grasping this truth gives us the perfect lens through which we can view the Old Testament, where we find some of the most challenging passages to comprehend. Be confident in this, that our God is merciful, compassionate, slow to get angry, and filled with unfailing love (Jonah 4:2). Reject any caricatures that try to box Him in as judgmental, angry, and violent.

1. Thank God for His Son Jesus and the gift He is to the world.
2. Thank God for His unfailing love that endures forever (Psalm 136).
3. Pray that you will always see God's actions and decisions through the same characteristics that you see in Jesus.
4. Pray that God will heal your heart of any misconceptions regarding His true nature.
5. Pray that everyone will see God as a loving Father.

DRAW: Reflection.

THE FATHER, THE SON, & THE HOLY SPIRIT

DAY 13

The Resurrection and the Life

"But God is so rich in mercy, and he loved us so much, that even though we were dead because of our sins, he gave us life when he raised Christ from the dead. (It is only by God's grace that you have been saved!)" — **Ephesians 2:4-5, NLT**

Although we were breathing, doing, and being, we were the walking dead. That's why Jesus said in John 10:10, "I came that they may have life, and have it abundantly." This is a powerful truth that stands in stark contrast to the misconception that Jesus came to make bad people good. He knew that no amount of good deeds could save us, that we would have to become new creations in Him. We would need to be beings who aren't just saved from sin, but dead to sin; and alive to God through Him (Romans 6:11). We were given this gift of salvation because of God's great love and kindness.

1. Thank God that He is kind and loves you greatly.
2. Thank God for saving you not by your works, but by His merciful kindness (Ephesians 2:8-9).
3. Ask God to help you experience the rich and satisfying life He promised (John 10:10).
4. Ask God to make you mindful that you are justified (made right with God) by the resurrection of the Lord Jesus, and not by what you can do.
5. Ask God to cleanse you from any old ways of thinking that would have you work for your right standing with God.

6. If you don't have a close relationship with Jesus, but want one, ask Him to help you know Him better.

7. Always remember that salvation is a gift. It's available to anyone, anywhere, in any condition, regardless of their past or present circumstances. Romans 10:9-10 explains clearly how God offers us this gift of eternal/resurrection life.

"If you confess with your mouth that Jesus is Lord [Jesus is my Master and Jesus is God] and believe in your heart that God raised him from the dead, you will be saved. For it is by believing in your heart that you are made right with God, and it is by confessing with your mouth that you are saved." — **Romans 10:9-10, NLT**

DRAW: Resurrection life.

The Father, the Son, & the Holy Spirit

DAY 14

The Father, The Son, & The Holy Spirit

Growing Closer
Discussion Questions

1. How did you feel after reading Job 38?

2. Why do you think God chose to respond to Job with a list of questions?

3. Has your communication with God changed since starting this section on the Father, the Son & the Holy Spirit? If yes, how?

4. Which person of the Godhead are you closer to, and why?

5. Which person of the Godhead do you want to build a closer relationship with, and why?

6. What steps are you going to take to develop this relationship?

"To love someone
means to see him
as God intended him."
— **Fyodor Dostoevsky**

Week 3

DAY 15

Love is Supernatural

"A new command I give you: Love one another. As I have loved you, so you must love one another." **— John 13:34, NIV**

Loving others as Christ loves us is a supernatural act. With our own strength, it is impossible to love as deeply and purely as God loves, because God is love (1 John 4:8).

1. Ask God to give you His supernatural love (Romans 5:5).
2. Pray that you will be quick to demonstrate His love, even in difficult situations, including with people you don't agree with.
3. Read 1 Corinthians 13:1-7 and in place of love, put your name.
4. Ask God to raise you up to the standard He has set for love in 1 Corinthians 13.

DRAW: Receiving love and sharing love.

LOVE & LOVED

DAY 16

Love Covers All

"Hatred stirs up strife, but love covers all transgressions."
— Proverbs 10:12, NASB

Love has the power to transform any situation, region, or person. Love is so powerful that it was the sole reason God sent His only Son, Jesus, to die in our place so that we might have everlasting life.

Even though we earned death as the payment due for our sins, God's love gifted us life (Romans 6:23). Despite being grieved by the evil and wicked state of man, God's love compelled Him to help us.

When we allow love to lead us, solutions are available for any situation that grieves our heart.

1. Thank God for the transforming power of love.
2. What injustice, social problem, or cause grieves your heart?
3. Ask God to intervene in the situation that grieves you.
4. Ask the Holy Spirit to let love reign so deeply in you that you are driven to action.
5. Ask God to show you how He wants you to participate in bringing about change in the situation that saddens you.
6. Pray that you won't be afraid to sacrifice.

DRAW: The issue that grieves you, transformed by love.

LOVE & LOVED

DAY 17

Love is Strong

"But you, Lord, are a compassionate and gracious God, slow to anger, abounding in love and faithfulness." — **Psalm 86:15, NIV**

1. Thank God for being compassionate.
2. Thank God for having care and concern for your life.
3. Thank God for being merciful, not punishing you as your sins deserve.
4. Thank God for His faithfulness toward you.
5. Thank God that He doesn't give up on you and He doesn't leave or abandon you.
6. Thank God that He accepts you before you behave.
7. Thank God that His love never fails you.

Write out the things that cause you to miss the mark (sin). Then create an image on top of it that represents God's love. As you create, ask God to permanently separate you from the things you wrote.

DRAW: Your sin, covered by God's love.

LOVE & LOVED

DAY 18

Love Chain

"Let love and faithfulness never leave you; bind them around your neck, write them on the tablet of your heart."
— Proverbs 3:3-4, NIV

1. Thank God for the ability to love and be faithful.
2. Thank God for giving you a new heart and putting a new spirit in you (Ezekiel 36:26).
3. Ask God to help you be faithful and love without concern of reciprocation.
4. Forgive those who have not reciprocated your love and faithfulness.
5. Ask God to help you be vulnerable.
6. Ask God to help you be strong in your commitment to His way of doing life.

DRAW: A love and faithfulness necklace.

LOVE & LOVED

DAY 19

God's Love

"But God demonstrates His own love toward us, in that while we were yet sinners, Christ died for us." — **Romans 5:8, NASB**

DRAW: A "God Thought" on this Scripture.
See page 21 for instructions.

LOVE & LOVED

DAY 20

Love Brings Rest

"The LORD your God is in your midst, a victorious warrior. He will exult over you with joy, He will be quiet in His love, He will rejoice over you with shouts of joy." — **Zephaniah 3:17, NASB**

DRAW: Soak in God's presence for 30 minutes. Let your ears listen to God's delight in you, let your face smile as you see God's celebration over you, let your mind be silenced by God's love, let your soul rest because of your victory.

LOVE & LOVED

DAY 21

LOVE & LOVED

Growing Closer
Discussion Questions

1. What does love look like?
2. Can we love apart from truth? Why or why not?
3. How do we know when we are being loved well?
4. How do you see God's love manifested in your life?
5. How are you cultivating a lifestyle of love?

"The confession of evil works is the first beginning of good works."
— **St. Augustine**

Week 4

DAY 22

Sin Separates

"If we confess our sins, He is faithful and righteous to forgive us our sins and to cleanse us from all unrighteousness."
— 1 John 1:9, NASB

Confess. Don't hold back. You are in a safe place with your Father. He calls you to come boldly before His throne of grace, so that you might receive mercy and help in your time of need (Hebrews 4:16).

Sin separates us from God. It causes a disruption in our fellowship with God and in the blessings we receive from Him. It never separates us from God's love, but it causes us not to be able to fully partake of the benefits of His love. That's why it's so important for us to live a lifestyle of sincere repentance, meaning we not only turn from sin, but we turn our hearts to God.

When we live a lifestyle of repentance, we are actively guarding the connection we have with God never allowing it to remain broken for any period of time. That's why true repentance is a lifestyle and not something we just do occasionally.

1. Take time to confess your sins and ask the Holy Spirit to reveal to you any sins you are unaware of.
2. Ask for forgiveness for all of your sins.
3. Take a moment to turn your affections toward God.
4. Thank your Papa for His goodness and faithfulness.
5. Thank God for cleansing you of all wrongfulness and unjust acts.

DRAW: Repentance.

CONFESS & REPENT

DAY 23

Forgive One Another

"For if you forgive other people when they sin against you, your heavenly Father will also forgive you." — **Matthew 6:14, NIV**

1. Thank God that He has given you the power to forgive others.
2. Take time to forgive the people who have harmed you.
3. Are you having a hard time forgiving someone? If so, who?
4. Ask God to break down the barriers between you and the other person.
5. Take note of where you are in this forgiveness process and make a commitment to bring it to completion, if you haven't already.
6. Thank your Papa that He is forgiving.
7. Ask your Father to forgive you, if you have forgiven others.

DRAW: A mended heart.

CONFESS & REPENT

DAY 24

Meekness

"Understand this, my dear brothers and sisters: You must all be quick to listen, slow to speak, and slow to get angry. Human anger does not produce the righteousness God desires. So get rid of all the filth and evil in your lives, and humbly accept the word God has planted in your hearts, for it has the power to save your souls." — **James 1:19-21, NLT**

1. What specific filth and evil do you need to remove from your life?
2. Ask the Holy Spirit to make all sin taste bitter, and only Christ sweet.
3. Ask God to remove everything that interferes with your relationship with Him.
4. The Word of God has the power to save our souls, if we receive it with meekness. Meekness is the opposite of self-assertiveness and self-interest. It stems from trust in God's goodness and control over every situation. Pray that you will live with complete trust in God's plan and goodness for your life.
5. Pray that you will apply God's Word to your life and not just hear it.
6. Pray that God's Word will be fully demonstrated in your life.

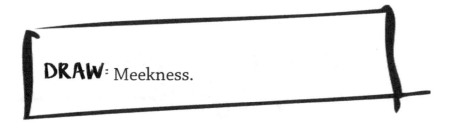

DRAW: Meekness.

CONFESS & REPENT

DAY 25

Freedom Speaks

"If you abide in my word, you are truly my disciples, and you will know the truth, and the truth will set you free."
— John 8:31-32, ESV

1. Where do you feel bound in your life?
2. Ask God to lead you to Scriptures that speak His truth regarding whatever you feel restricted or imprisoned by.
3. Pray the Scriptures God gives you over yourself.
4. Ask Jesus to break every chain, every lie, and every doubt off your life.
5. Thank Jesus for setting you free (John 8:36).

DRAW: Lock and key.

Challenge: Use only a pen.

CONFESS & REPENT

DAY 26

Guard Your Heart

"Above all else, guard your heart, for everything you do flows from it. Keep your mouth free of perversity; keep corrupt talk far from your lips. Let your eyes look straight ahead; fix your gaze directly before you. Give careful thought to the paths for your feet and be steadfast in all your ways. Do not turn to the right or the left; keep your foot from evil." **— Proverbs 4:23-27, NIV**

1. Do your words, actions, and responses show that they come from a heart that is well guarded? Why or why not?

2. Proverbs 4:24-27 explains how to guard your heart. Which of these techniques are you currently using?

3. Ask God to help you put into practice the daily act of guarding your heart.

4. Ask God to show you any places in your heart that are open to ungodly influences.

5. Pray for your heart to be purged from the works and effects of any ungodly influences.

6. Pray that those openings are closed and shut up tight with God's provision and love.

DRAW: A well guarded heart.

CONFESS & REPENT

DAY 21

Weakness

"In the same way, the Spirit helps us in our weakness. We do not know what we ought to pray for, but the Spirit himself intercedes for us through wordless groans. And he who searches our hearts knows the mind of the Spirit, because the Spirit intercedes for God's people in accordance with the will of God."
— Romans 8:26-27, NIV

When we don't know what to pray, the Holy Spirit prays for us through our sighs and moans. Our cries become Spirit-led prayers that line up with God's will for our lives and the issues that grieve us.

1. Thank the Holy Spirit for helping you in your weakness.

2. Thank the Holy Spirit for guiding your prayers when you don't know God's will regarding an issue or lack the capacity to make sense of your experiences.

3. Write down the issues that you want to pray about, but you aren't sure what to say.

4. Ask the Holy Spirit to intercede for you according to God's will regarding the issues you identified above.

5. When we are flustered or confused, sometimes words fail us and a sigh or a groan is all that we can muster. If this describes your current situation, let out a groan or a sigh.

DRAW: Wordless prayer.

CONFESS & REPENT

DAY 28

CONFESS & REPENT

Growing Closer
Discussion Questions

1. How do you feel after a week of concentrated confession and repentance?

2. Did you gain any tools or learn anything useful to help you in the future? If so, what?

3. What role does confession play in the healing of past wounds?

4. In James 5:16, we are instructed to confess our sins to other believers. Have you ever followed this teaching? If so, what was the outcome and how did you feel?

5. How would you respond if someone needed to confess a sin to you?

6. How could you prepare yourself for such an occurrence?

"The waters are rising, but so am I. I am not going under, but over."
— **Catherine Booth**

Week 5

DAY 29

Impossible Situations

"Jesus looked at them and said, 'With man this is impossible, but with God all things are possible.'" — **Matthew 19:26, NIV**

1. What challenges are you facing that you believe God can turn into amazing opportunities?
2. Ask God to give you victory in every impossible situation.
3. Pray for strength and courage in the midst of the problems.
4. Pray for God's direction and wisdom.
5. Ask God to help you partner with Him to overcome every challenge that comes your way.
6. Listen for your first instructional word from your Father.
7. Take courage; Jesus has already overcome, and so will you (John 16:33).

DRAW: Winning in the storm.

PROTECTION & PROVISION

DAY 30

■ ■■■■ ■ ■ ■■■ ■ ■■ ■ ■■■ ■

Armor of God

"Therefore, put on every piece of God's armor so you will be able to resist the enemy in the time of evil. Then after the battle you will still be standing firm. Stand your ground, putting on the belt of truth and the body armor of God's righteousness. For shoes, put on the peace that comes from the Good News so that you will be fully prepared. In addition to all of these, hold up the shield of faith to stop the fiery arrows of the devil. Put on salvation as your helmet, and take the sword of the Spirit, which is the word of God." — **Ephesians 6:13-17, NLT**

Paul wrote in his letter to the Romans, "Put on the armor ... clothe yourselves with the Lord Jesus Christ" (Romans 13:12-14). When we put on the armor of God, we are putting on the Lord Jesus Christ Himself. According to Matthew Henry, we put Him on as Lord to rule us, as Jesus to save us, and as Christ, anointed and appointed by the Father to do this ruling, saving work. If we are to make a successful stand against the enemy, we must do it in Christ, fully covered in the armor of God. Therefore we must ask ourselves, are we fully covered, or are we missing pieces?

1. Underline all the pieces of God's armor mentioned in the passage above (Ephesians 6:13-17).
2. Are you fully covered or are you missing pieces of God's armor?
3. Ask God what piece(s) of the armor He wants to give you today.

4. Ask Him why He wants to give you each specific piece.
5. Put on the armor. How do you feel?
6. Thank God for His armor and His care for you.

DRAW: The armor you received and the reason.

PROTECTION & PROVISION

DAY 31

Song of Victory

"For you are my hiding place; you protect me from trouble. You surround me with songs of victory." — **Psalm 32:7, NLT**

1. Thank God that He is your hiding place.
2. Thank God that in Him you are taken care of.
3. Thank God that He protects you from trouble.
4. Thank God that no weapon formed against you will prevail (Isaiah 54:17).
5. Thank your Papa for His encouragement.
6. Ask God to reveal one victory song that surrounds you.
7. Take time to listen.
8. Write down what you hear.

DRAW: Your victory song.

Challenge: Sing this song over yourself everyday for the next 24 days.

PROTECTION & PROVISION

DAY 32

Relax

"Be still, and know that I am God! I will be honored by every nation. I will be honored throughout the world."
— Psalm 46:10, NLT

In other words, God is saying, "RELAX! Let go and know (find out) that I am ruler and judge."

Sometimes we forget that even with all of our effort and brilliant ideas, they might still not be enough to solve the complex issues in our lives. But there's hope. God always has an answer for impossible situations. He is ruler and judge and therefore He can decree a thing and it happens. In the end, God will be honored and His enemies will be scattered.

1. What do you need to let go of and leave in the capable hands of God?
2. Ask God to show you the issue(s) that He wants to take off your shoulders.
3. Pray for the faith to trust that God will work it out for your good—without your advice.

DRAW: Cease striving.

Challenge: Use only two colors and create a quick drawing with your eyes closed.

PROTECTION & PROVISION

DAY 33

You Have the Victory

"For the LORD your God is going with you! He will fight for you against your enemies, and he will give you victory!"
— Deuteronomy 20:4, NLT

1. Listen to your favorite victory song.
2. Rejoice in the fact that God gives you victory over all your enemies (Ephesians 6:12).
3. Sing, dance, shout, and give thanks!

DRAW: A brain full of God's good report for your life.

PROTECTION & PROVISION

DAY 34

He Who Calls, Supplies

"God's work done in God's way will never lack God's supplies."
— Hudson Taylor

1. Thank God for His provision.
2. Thank God for His instruction.
3. Pray that you will always focus on God's unlimited riches when planning, dreaming, casting vision, setting goals or facing challenges.
4. Pray Philippians 4:19 over yourself.
5. Ask your Father to show you His unlimited supply of provision.

"And this same God who takes care of me will supply all your needs from his glorious riches, which have been given to us in Christ Jesus." **— Philippians 4:19, NLT**

DRAW: A storehouse full of God's supplies for your life.

PROTECTION & PROVISION

DAY 35

PROTECTION & PROVISION

Growing Closer
Discussion Questions

1. What type of situations cause you to doubt God's protection and provision?

2. How do you respond when faced with these situations?

3. How should you respond when faced with these situations?

4. How has your song of victory impacted your week?

5. Which piece(s) of armor did God give you? Have you noticed a difference in your well-being?

6. Do you feel that you are currently being protected and provided for? Why or why not?

7. Let those who can see God's provision and protection pray for those who need breakthrough in this area.

"Should we not press it home upon our consciences that the sole object of our conversion was not the salvation of our own souls, but that we might become co-workers with our Lord and Master in the conversion of the world?"

— **Lottie Moon**

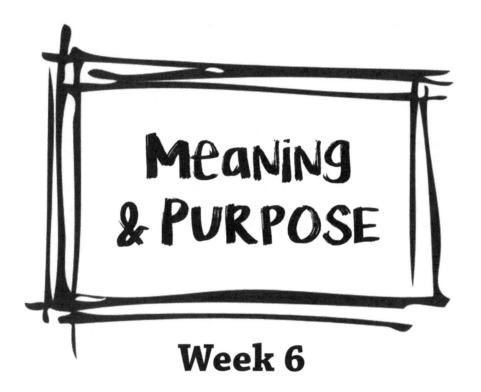

Week 6

DAY 36

God's Call, God's Command

"But now, O Jacob, listen to the LORD who created you. O Israel, the one who formed you says, 'Do not be afraid, for I have ransomed you. I have called you by name; you are mine.'"
— **Isaiah 43:1, NLT**

Israel's birth name was Jacob, but God gave him a new name in Genesis 32:28. In that moment, God changed his name from "trickster, supplanter, heel grabber" to "soldier of God."

1. Thank God that He calls you by name.
2. Ask the Lord if He has a new name for you.
3. If yes, what's your name? If no, what name does the Lord call you by?
4. Thank God that He has a word of encouragement for you today.
5. God commanded Israel not to be afraid. What is He commanding you?

DRAW: Who has the Lord called you? What has the Lord commanded you?

MEANING & PURPOSE

DAY 31

Father's Voice

"And a voice from Heaven said, 'This is my Son, whom I love; with him I am well pleased.'" — **Matthew 3:17, NIV**

1. Thank God that His thoughts toward you are precious and plentiful (Psalm 139:17-18 and Jeremiah 29:11).

2. What is the Father speaking over you?

DRAW: Create a Mind Map around the single concept of "God's thoughts about me." Start by drawing this concept as an image in the center of a blank page. See page 19 for further instructions on how to draw a Mind Map.

MEANING & PURPOSE

DAY 38

A Listening Ear

"I will instruct you and teach you in the way which you should go; I will counsel you with My eye upon you." — **Psalm 32:8, NASB**

God wants to guide us along the best path for our lives with His counsel and teaching (Psalm 32:8). That's why it's important for us to have a listening ear. We need to be able to receive instructions from our Creator because He formed us with purpose. Ephesians 2:10 tells us that long ago, before we were born, He preplanned good works for us to do. He has chosen in His infinite wisdom not to instantly download to us everything that we will do in this life, or everything we will become, but rather form us moment by moment into the people we are to be, and lead us into the experiences we are to have. This process is purpose.

Often, we think of purpose as a destination, but in actuality, it's a journey. We live that journey out through an intimate relationship with our Creator, receiving our instructions as we go.

1. Thank God for His counsel and direction.
2. Thank God for ordering your steps (Psalm 37:23).
3. Pray for your ears to be finely tuned to only hear the voice of God your Father.
4. Pray that you would be obedient to the voice of God.

DRAW: A listening ear. What do you hear?

MEANING & PURPOSE

DAY 39

Identity

"But you are a chosen race, a royal priesthood, a holy nation, a people for God's own possession, so that you may proclaim the excellencies of Him who has called you out of darkness into His marvelous light." — **1 Peter 2:9, NASB**

God gives us the amazing privilege of making His greatness known throughout the earth. When we accept His invitation to know Him and to fellowship with Him, we escape a lifestyle of sin and receive the great honor of becoming His children and partnering with Him to show the world His goodness and love.

1. Thank God for calling you out of a lifestyle of sin (darkness).
2. Thank God for inviting you into relationship with Him (light).
3. Thank God that your identity is found only in Him.
4. Thank God that your identity isn't found in your career or your possessions.
5. In 1 Peter 2:9, God reveals to us some foundational truths about our identities. Are you walking in the fullness of who God has already said you are?

    • A Chosen Race – A member of a family that has a different spirit than the world

    • A Royal Priest – An intercessor for others

    • A Holy Nation – A member of a community that loves God and obeys Him

- God's Possession – His child

6. Identify the places where you need to grow, and pray that the Holy Spirit will help you become all that God has called you to be.

DRAW: A coat of arms (a shield) and include the four characteristics listed in today's Scripture, and at least one characteristic specific to you.

MEANING & PURPOSE

DAY 40

Be Unashamed

"One night the Lord spoke to Paul in a vision and told him, 'Don't be afraid! Speak out! Don't be silent!'" — **Acts 18:9, NLT**

1. Ask the Holy Spirit to give you or confirm the message He wants you to speak.
2. What is He saying?
3. Pray that you are fueled by God's love to declare this message boldly.
4. Pray that you are filled with conviction and boldness.

To be unashamed and to be bold doesn't mean we have to be rude. It doesn't mean that we disconnect from the world or condemn the world. For God didn't send his Son into the world to condemn the world, but to save the world through Him (John 3:17). We are to be ambassadors of Christ, pleading with people to be reunited with God (2 Corinthians 5:20).

Ambassadors are official diplomats sent by a leader to represent them abroad. Christ has appointed us to represent Him in the Earth and just like any good ambassador we are to represent Him in our temperament, in our actions, and in our words.

The Scriptures tell us that when we do this work of reconciliation, it's as if God is making His appeal through us. Always remember that at the heart of God when He launched this rescue mission was love (John 3:16).

DRAW: What does the world look like as a result of you fearlessly declaring the message God gave you?

MEANING & PURPOSE

DAY 41

Success vs. Failure

"Now Joseph had been taken down to Egypt; and Potiphar, an Egyptian officer of Pharaoh, the captain of the bodyguard, bought him from the Ishmaelites, who had taken him down there. The LORD was with Joseph, so he became a successful man. And he was in the house of his master, the Egyptian."
— **Genesis 39:1-2, NASB**

Joseph was a slave in Potiphar's house, yet God caused him to be successful.

1. Ask the Father what He considers success.
2. Ask Him what He considers failure.
3. Be sure to write down His responses.
4. Pray that you will have the character to handle success and perceived delays.
5. Pray that you will have success despite your circumstances and despite opposition.
6. Thank God for your journey and your success.

DRAW: Success.

Meaning & Purpose

DAY 42

MEANING & PURPOSE

Growing Closer
Discussion Questions

1. Read Proverbs 30:21-23 and discuss the overall theme/message of this passage.

2. Why is identity and purpose so important to the human experience?

3. What's the relationship between identity and purpose?

4. How can knowing your identity help you to prosper financially, socially, emotionally, mentally, and spiritually?

5. Have you gone through a season where you struggled with identity? If so, how did you overcome it?

6. Are you currently going through a season where you feel lost and unsure about your future? If yes, ask for advice and receive prayer for breakthrough in this area.

"I rise today in the power of Christ's birth and baptism, in the power of his crucifixion and burial, in the power of his rising and ascending, in the power of his descending and judging. I rise today."
— **St. Patrick's Breastplate**

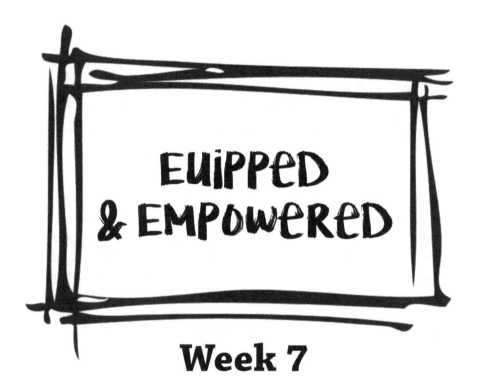

Week 7

DAY 43

Be Filled

"Don't be drunk with wine, because that will ruin your life. Instead, be filled with the Holy Spirit, singing psalms and hymns and spiritual songs among yourselves, and making music to the Lord in your hearts." — **Ephesians 5:18-19, NLT**

Just as someone can be under the influence of alcohol and their mind and body responds to that stimulus, as Christians we are to be under the influence of the Holy Spirit. To be filled with the Holy Spirit is to have every area of our lives under the Spirit's control. This isn't forced upon us. We must make conscious decisions to surrender to the leading of the Holy Spirit moment by moment. It's a choice.

Colossians 3:16 tells us that God's Word helps us live out a Spirit-filled life, if we read the Scriptures and apply the teaching to our lives.

1. Ask the Holy Spirit to fill you up and take control over every part of your life.
2. Ask the Holy Spirit to fill your lips with spiritual songs and your heart with music to the Lord.
3. Ask the Holy Spirit to give you a great hunger for God's Word.
4. Ask the Holy Spirit to make you a hearer and doer of the Word.
5. Thank the Holy Spirit for filling you.
6. Thank God for the ability to be thankful.

DRAW: Overflowing.

EQUIPPED & EMPOWERED

DAY 44

★ ★ ★ ★ ★ ★ ★ ★ ★ ★ ★

Miracle Worker

"And these signs will accompany those who believe: In my name they will drive out demons; they will speak in new tongues; they will pick up snakes with their hands; and when they drink deadly poison, it will not hurt them at all; they will place their hands on sick people, and they will get well." — **Mark 16:17-18, NIV**

To be the miracle workers that we were called to be, we must be willing to take risks and exercise our authority in the earth. Luke 10:19 tells us that Jesus has given us authority over all the power of the enemy. This includes authority over illnesses and destructive mindsets. The only way we will see the change we hope for is to combine our belief in God's truth with a lifestyle of unashamed risks (James 2:17).

1. What thoughts come to mind after reading these Scriptures?
2. Do you see these signs following you or other believers you know? Why or why not?
3. Pray that you will use your God-given authority to release the power of God in the earth.
4. Ask God to give you a new level of extreme faith matched by extreme obedience.
5. Ask God to bring you into the fullness of everything that Jesus paid for with His blood.
6. Ask the Holy Spirit to help you live out your calling as a miracle worker and do the things Jesus said you would do in Mark 16:17-18.

7. Thank God that He has already given you the power and the authority to be a world changer and a history maker in His name and for His glory.

DRAW: The supernatural.

EQUIPPED & EMPOWERED

DAY 45

★ ★ ★ ★ ★ ★ ★ ★ ★ ★ ★

Practice, Practice, Practice

"This is why I remind you to fan into flames the spiritual gift God gave you when I laid my hands on you." — **2 Timothy 1:6, NLT**

1. Ask God to show you what gifts He has given you. What did He say? (For examples from Scripture, see Romans 12:6-7, 1 Corinthians 12:8-10 and 12:28, Ephesians 4:11, and 1 Peter 4:10-11.)

2. Are you using the gifts God gave you? If not, what changes do you plan to make moving forward?

DRAW: Create an image that will remind you to fan into flames/stir up/steward the specific gifts God has given you.

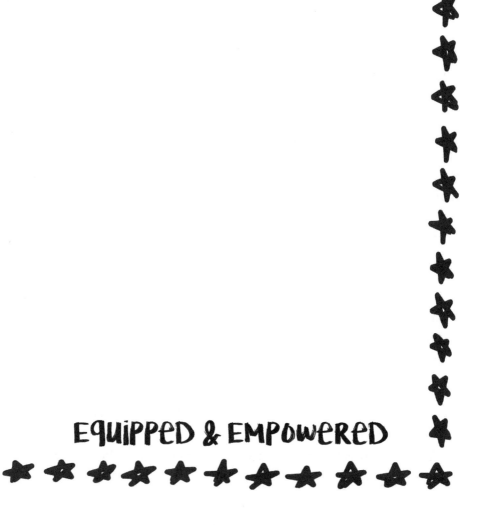

EQUIPPED & EMPOWERED

DAY 46

Stay Focused

"Peter said to Him, 'Lord, if it is You, command me to come to You on the water.' And He said, 'Come!' And Peter got out of the boat, and walked on the water and came toward Jesus. But seeing the wind, he became frightened, and beginning to sink, he cried out, 'Lord, save me!' Immediately Jesus stretched out His hand and took hold of him, and said to him, 'You of little faith, why did you doubt?'" — **Matthew 14:28-31, NASB**

When Peter had his eyes fixed on Jesus, he was able to walk on water. He only began to sink once he became focused on the circumstances that surrounded him. Those circumstances began to challenge his faith in Jesus' Word.

If you stay focused on Jesus and remain in a place of faith, nothing that God has called you to do will be impossible for you.

1. Thank God for allowing you to do the impossible when your focus is on Jesus.
2. Pray that you won't doubt, but would remain full of faith as you do the impossible.
3. Pray that the concerns of this world will not distract you from Jesus.
4. Thank God that Jesus holds the solutions to everything that concerns you.
5. What is one risk you want to take that God has called you to do?
6. Stay focused on Jesus and do it.

DRAW: Focus.

Challenge: Use only a pencil.

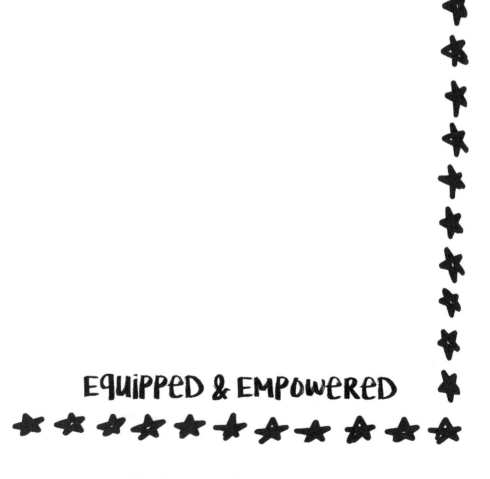

EQUIPPED & EMPOWERED

DAY 47

★ ★ ★ ★ ★ ★ ★ ★ ★ ★ ★

Know Mysteries

"Ask me and I will tell you remarkable secrets you do not know about things to come." — **Jeremiah 33:3, NLT**

Apart from God, we know next to nothing. But because of our exalted status as God's children, we can know mysteries. In this Scripture, God invites us to ask Him about the future.

1. Ask God one question.
2. Take time to listen to God's response.

DRAW: A newspaper with a headline story of God's response.

EQUIPPED & EMPOWERED

DAY 48

✦ ✦ ✦ ✦ ✦ ✦ ✦ ✦ ✦ ✦ ✦

Clothe Yourself

"Since God chose you to be the holy people he loves, you must clothe yourselves with tenderhearted mercy, kindness, humility, gentleness, and patience. Make allowance for each other's faults, and forgive anyone who offends you. Remember, the Lord forgave you, so you must forgive others. Above all, clothe yourselves with love, which binds us all together in perfect harmony."
— Colossians 3:12-14, NLT

1. Thank God for choosing you and loving you.
2. Underline the six characteristics that God wants you to clothe yourself with.
3. Highlight the qualities you do well.
4. Circle the qualities you want to grow in.
5. Pray for the full expression of all of the qualities in your life. Be specific!
6. Pray for unity in the body of Christ.

DRAW: Clothe yourself with tenderhearted mercy, kindness, humility, gentleness, patience, and love.

EQUIPPED & EMPOWERED

DAY 49

EQUIPPED & EMPOWERED

Growing Closer
Discussion Questions

1. After reading Mark 16:17-18, how do you feel about Jesus' statement that believers should be accompanied by miracles?

2. What are some obstacles to applying this verse to your life?

3. What steps are you taking to position yourself to lead a life of miracles?

4. Have you had a miracle happen in your life? If yes, please share.

5. Have you ever performed a miracle? If yes, please share.

6. How important are miracles in spreading the gospel?

"Sympathy is no substitute for action."
— **David Livingstone**

Week 8

DAY 50

Disturb Us, Lord

Disturb us, Lord, when
We are too well pleased with ourselves,
When our dreams have come true
Because we have dreamed too little,
When we arrived safely
Because we sailed too close to the shore.

Disturb us, Lord, when
With the abundance of things we possess
We have lost our thirst
For the waters of life;
Having fallen in love with life,
We have ceased to dream of eternity
And in our efforts to build a new earth,
We have allowed our vision
Of the new Heaven to dim.

Disturb us, Lord, to dare more boldly,
To venture on wider seas
Where storms will show your mastery;
Where losing sight of land,
We shall find the stars.
We ask You to push back
The horizons of our hopes;
And to push into the future
In strength, courage, hope, and love.

— Sir Francis Drake, 1577

1. Ask God to make you uncomfortable.
2. Ask God to increase your passion for eternity.
3. Ask God to give you bigger and more daring dreams.
4. Ask God to deposit a hope in you for heaven.
5. Ask God to give you boldness.
6. Ask God to give you a hunger for His kingdom to come and His will be done on earth as it is in Heaven.
7. Thank God for answering your prayers.
8. Thank God for the ability to dream bigger.

DRAW: Disturb me, Lord.

Challenge: Use paper collage.

UNleaSheD & ReleaSeD

DAY 51

Be Adventurous

"Have I not commanded you? Be strong and courageous! Do not be afraid; do not be discouraged, for the Lord your God will be with you wherever you go." — **Joshua 1:9, NIV**

1. Thank God that He is with you wherever you go.
2. Ask God to make you strong and courageous.
3. Rebuke the spirit of discouragement.
4. Thank God for the journey ahead.
5. Ask God to show you what your adventure with Him will look like.

DRAW: An adventure with God.

UNleashed & ReleaseD

DAY 52

Send Me, Lord

"And how will anyone go and tell them without being sent? That is why the Scriptures say, 'How beautiful are the feet of messengers who bring good news!'" — **Romans 10:15, NLT**

1. Jesus commands you to go and make disciples of all peoples (Matthew 28:18-20). Where do you want to go (e.g., sphere of influence, country, region, school)?

2. Ask God where He wants you to go.

3. Is it the same place?

4. If the place is different, take time to talk with God about the difference.

5. Ask God to send you out.

6. Pray that you aren't sidetracked by the comforts of this world.

7. Pray that you serve from God's love and not for God's love.

8. Pray that you serve from a place of victory and not for victory.

9. Pray that you rest in God's promises and His perfect timing.

DRAW: Envelope(s) addressed to the place(s) that you are being sent. Pray out loud for those places and for the people in those places. Pray for their peace. Pray that they receive the news of Jesus Christ as Lord and God's love for them with their whole heart, mind, and soul. These places can include countries, cities, people groups, industries, schools, agencies, etc.

UNleaShed & ReIeaSeD

DAY 53

Finish Your Race

"I have fought the good fight, I have finished the race, and I have remained faithful. And now the prize awaits me—the crown of righteousness, which the Lord, the righteous Judge, will give me on the day of his return. And the prize is not just for me but for all who eagerly look forward to his appearing."
— 2 Timothy 4:7-8, NLT

1. Thank God for His Spirit that will enable you to finish your race (Philippians 1:6).
2. Thank God that He judges well and correctly.
3. Pray that you will remain faithful and finish your race.
4. Pray that you will receive your crown of righteousness.
5. Pray that everyone who follows Jesus will also finish well.
6. Pray that you become and remain eager and excited about Jesus coming to the earth again (Acts 1:11 and Revelation 20:1-6).

DRAW: A crown of righteousness.

UNLEASHED & RELEASED

DAY 54

Get Wisdom & Understanding

"The beginning of wisdom is: Acquire wisdom; And with all your acquiring, get understanding." — **Proverbs 4:7, NASB**

Wisdom is knowing how to apply knowledge. It's knowing precisely what to do with what you already know.

Understanding is the ability to perceive (become aware or conscious of) and discern a situation properly.

1. Thank God that He gives wisdom generously to anyone who asks (James 1:5).
2. Ask God to give you wisdom.
3. Ask God to give you understanding (discernment) regarding every aspect of your life.
4. You've been on an eight-week adventure with your Papa. This is a good time to reflect on your journey. Ask Him what piece of wisdom He wants you to take away from this experience. Sum up God's response into a title for your journal.

DRAW: Decorate the cover of your journal with the title.

UNLEASHED & RELEASED

DAY 55

Get a Vision

"Where there is no prophetic vision the people cast off restraint, but blessed is he who keeps the law." — **Proverbs 29:18, ESV**

We need God's vision for our lives. Otherwise, we will do what we think is right based upon limited information, and that will always turn out badly. When we become the leaders of our lives, we put ourselves at a big disadvantage. We go from allowing an all-knowing, all-seeing, all-wise, all-powerful, loving, and kind God to lead us, to a finite, short-sighted, emotionally unstable, sinful human being—also known as us—take charge of our lives. Scary, right?

1. Thank God for His leadership and guidance in your life.
2. Ask your Papa to give you a glimpse into the future He has for you.
3. Ask God to show you the next step He wants you to take on this journey.
4. Ask God to help you respond to His guidance with quick obedience.

DRAW: The vision you received, on the back cover of your journal.

UNleasheD & ReleaseD

DAY 56

UNleashed & Released

Growing Closer
Discussion Questions

1. What challenged you the most during the past eight weeks?

2. What was the most beautiful lesson you learned, or experience you had, during the past eight weeks?

3. What vision did you receive on Day 55 regarding your next step?

4. Review your fruit tree from Day 1. Which fruits do you see growing in your life?

5. Describe how your relationship with God has matured or changed.

Epilogue

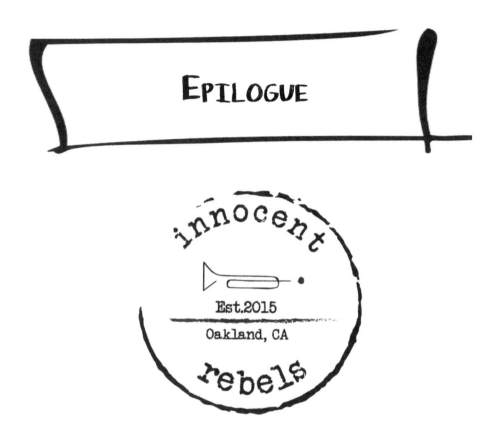

innocent rebels teaches Christians how to interrupt anyone's day with the supernatural because everyone needs a God encounter.

We believe that it is important to embrace a lifestyle of risk to show people that Jesus cares and loves them outrageously.

Find out more and get connected by visiting www.innocentrebels.com.

Review

Thank you for reading *Draw Near to Me*. I pray that this creative devotional journal has been a life-changing experience for you. It's my hope to get this book into the hands of as many people as possible. Gaining exposure as an independent author relies mostly on word-of-mouth, so if you have the time and inclination, please consider leaving a short review wherever you can. It really does make a difference. Thank you.